Keep~life~simple
Therapy

Keep~life~simple Therapy

written by
Linus Mundy

illustrated by
R.W. Alley

ONE
CARING
PLACE

Abbey Press

Text © 1993 Linus Mundy
Illustrations © 1993 St. Meinrad Archabbey
Published by One Caring Place
Abbey Press
St. Meinrad, Indiana 47577

Library of Congress Catalog Number
92-75341

ISBN 0-87029-257-9

Printed in the United States of America

Foreword

Life is a complicated affair. Too much to do; too little time. Too many demands; too few resources. Too much commotion and busy-ness; too little peace and quiet.

The answer? *An* answer: Choosing to reduce life to its essence and keep it simple (or, at least, simpler). The fruits of this choice (and really it is hundreds of *little* choices rather than one big one) are substantial:

- By living more simply, we free up our overtaxed personal resources—our minds, our emotions, our spirits—from anxiety.
- By living more simply, we free up some of our world's relentlessly overtaxed natural resources.
- By living more simply, we shorten our list of "stuff" to care about, which gives us the chance to care *more* about what (and whom) is left.
- By living more simply, we open up our hearts to receive and be one with our "Supernatural Resource," our God who loves us and wants— very simply—only our good.

If you yearn to experience how less can be more, let *Keep-life-simple Therapy* be your gentle guide to what is truly essential.

1.

Reduce life to its essence. It is mostly love that matters...and lasts.

2.

Reduce love to its essence. It is mostly a knowing and a being known. Make the effort, do the work, of getting to know and letting your true self be known. You will see the oneness of love and Love.

3.

Learn the art of saying "no."
When you <u>ex</u>clude something,
you invariably <u>in</u>clude
something else even more
fully.

4.

Welcome your role in the drama of creation. Imagine the part you play as a leading role (which it is). But once in a while, keep still and let God speak the parts.

5.

Celebrate the ordinary. Your heart knows the comfort and the beauty in common things. Let it tell your head.

6.

Don't expect so much from <u>more</u>—and so little from <u>less</u>. Expect a lot from <u>less</u>. You won't be disappointed.

7.

It is hard to know when you "have enough." Make the question "Do I really need more?" part of your life's work.

8.

Look to nature for nurture. It is as reliable as the God who provides it.

9.

When making choices, opt for the plain, the simple, the functional. Less goes wrong when you stick to life's standard equipment.

10.

Do not pretend to be anything you are not. That way you can always be consistent and truly free.

11.

Live in time. Rushing to get one thing over so you can move on to something "more important" is folly.

12.

Practice being content. It is both the work and the reward of a lifetime.

13.

There is a time for doing—and a time for doing nothing. Don't underestimate the value of porch-sitting and rocking-chairing. They are simple gifts you can give to yourself—and others.

14.

Live intentionally. Forget that
and your life will be lived for
you.

15.

Learn to value spiritual things over material things. They last longer, cost less, bring more.

16.

Let manual labor, hard work, be a part of your life. You'll be proud of how humble it makes you.

17.

Be small and child-like. There is no simpler, better way to see the big picture.

18.

Try to eat and live lower on the food and resources chain. You'll be doing a world of good to beings yet unborn.

19.

Silence is golden. Seek it and it will quietly enrich your life.

20.

Get alone. It is one sure way of getting yourself together.

21.

Trust that God supplies you with unlimited good. There is grain left in the field even after the harvest.

22.

Remember that the primary reward of work is finding meaning and well-being, not money. Forget that and you'll stop being well.

23.

Set your desk, your chair, your sink, your sights with a view to the great outdoors. Life is simpler out there.

24.

Don't take your life too seriously. Trust in a God who cares for your every need.

25.

Don't let work and play be rivals. While each may have its separate place at times, both can also occupy the same space.

26.

Know your limits. There is nothing more freeing—or more motivating—than knowing what you can and cannot do well.

27.

Learn from life's oldest living things: trees. They impressively break forth with buds and colors—but know innately when it's time to shut down and be unimpressive.

28.

Strive to have access <u>to</u> things, not ownership <u>of</u> them. Possess something and it possesses you.

THE ESMÉ

29.

Create a ten-second wildflower meadow in your mind whenever you need it. Your imagination can be a great peacemaker in times of chaos.

30.

Think small. Planting tiny seeds in the small space given to you can change the whole world— or, at the very least, your view of it.

31.

Cultivate the simple virtue of patience. Anticipation is not the only reward for waiting.

32.

Don't forget that the longing for simplicity is a spiritual longing. Asking physical things to meet spiritual needs doesn't work.

33.

Do only one thing at a time. Putting yourself wholeheartedly into what you are doing—no matter how small or mundane—honors it…and you…and your Creator.

34.

Rediscover the joy of a quiet conversation, a simple story or game, an honest expression of affection for another. These simple gifts and pleasures will help keep your life balanced.

35.

Know that your true home is in the holy Presence. It's that simple. Don't wait for your calendar to be empty, or your permanent address to change, before recognizing that reality.

Linus Mundy is director of One Caring Place/Publications at Abbey Press. He has also written *Prayer-Walking*, *Slow-down Therapy*, *Finding Peace of Heart* and has contributed to *Grief Therapy*. He lives with his wife and three children in Santa Claus, Indiana.

Illustrator for the Abbey Press Elf-help Books, **R.W. Alley** also illustrates and writes children's books. He lives in Barrington, Rhode Island, with his wife, daughter, and son.

The Story of the Abbey Press Elves

The engaging figures that populate the Abbey Press "elf-help" line of publications and products first appeared in 1987 on the pages of a small self-help book called *Be-good-to-yourself Therapy*. Shaped by the publishing staff's vision and defined in R.W. Alley's inventive illustrations, they lived out author Cherry Hartman's gentle, self-nurturing advice with charm, poignancy, and humor.

Reader response was so enthusiastic that more Elf-help Books were soon under way, a still-growing series that has inspired a line of related gift products.

The especially endearing character featured in the early books—sporting a cap with a mood-changing candle in its peak—has since been joined by a spirited female elf with flowers in her hair.

These two exuberant, sensitive, resourceful, kindhearted, lovable sprites, along with their lively elfin community, reveal what's truly important as they offer messages of joy and wonder, playfulness and co-creation, wholeness and serenity, the miracle of life and the mystery of God's love.

With wisdom and whimsy, these little creatures with long noses demonstrate the elf-help way to a rich and fulfilling life.

Elf-help Books

...adding "a little character" and a lot of help to self-help reading!

Trust-in-God Therapy
#20119 $4.95   ISBN 0-87029-322-2

Elf-help for Overcoming Depression
#20134 $4.95   ISBN 0-87029-315-X

New Baby Therapy
#20140 $4.95   ISBN 0-87029-307-9

Grief Therapy for Men
#20141 $4.95   ISBN 0-87029-306-0

Living From Your Soul
#20146 $4.95   ISBN 0-87029-303-6

Teacher Therapy
#20145 $4.95   ISBN 0-87029-302-8

Be-good-to-your-family Therapy
#20154 $4.95   ISBN 0-87029-300-1

Stress Therapy
#20153 $4.95   ISBN 0-87029-301-X

Making-sense-out-of-suffering Therapy
#20156 $4.95   ISBN 0-87029-296-X

Get Well Therapy
#20157 $4.95   ISBN 0-87029-297-8

Anger Therapy
#20127 $4.95   ISBN 0-87029-292-7

Caregiver Therapy
#20164 $4.95   ISBN 0-87029-285-4

Self-esteem Therapy
#20165 $4.95   ISBN 0-87029-280-3

Take-charge-of-your-life Therapy
#20168 $4.95   ISBN 0-87029-271-4

Work Therapy
#20166 $4.95   ISBN 0-87029-276-5

Everyday-courage Therapy
#20167 $4.95   ISBN 0-87029-274-9

Peace Therapy
#20176 $4.95   ISBN 0-87029-273-0

Friendship Therapy
#20174 $4.95   ISBN 0-87029-270-6

Christmas Therapy (color edition)
#20175 $5.95   ISBN 0-87029-268-4

Grief Therapy
#20178 $4.95   ISBN 0-87029-267-6

More Be-good-to-yourself Therapy
#20180 $3.95   ISBN 0-87029-262-5

Happy Birthday Therapy
#20181 $4.95   ISBN 0-87029-260-9

Forgiveness Therapy
#20184 $4.95   ISBN 0-87029-258-7

Keep-life-simple Therapy
#20185 $4.95   ISBN 0-87029-257-9

Be-good-to-your-body Therapy
#20188 $4.95   ISBN 0-87029-255-2

Celebrate-your-womanhood Therapy
#20189 $4.95   ISBN 0-87029-254-4

Acceptance Therapy (color edition)
#20182 $5.95   ISBN 0-87029-259-5

Acceptance Therapy
#20190 $4.95   ISBN 0-87029-245-5

Keeping-up-your-spirits Therapy
#20195 $4.95   ISBN 0-87029-242-0

Play Therapy
#20200 $4.95   ISBN 0-87029-233-1

Slow-down Therapy
#20203 $4.95   ISBN 0-87029-229-3

One-day-at-a-time Therapy
#20204 $4.95   ISBN 0-87029-228-5

Prayer Therapy
#20206 $4.95   ISBN 0-87029-225-0

Be-good-to-your-marriage Therapy
#20205 $4.95   ISBN 0-87029-224-2

Be-good-to-yourself Therapy (hardcover)
#20196 $10.95   ISBN 0-87029-243-9

Be-good-to-yourself Therapy
#20255 $4.95   ISBN 0-87029-209-9

Available at your favorite bookstore or directly from
us at: One Caring Place, Abbey Press Publications
St. Meinrad, IN 47577. Or call 1-800-325-2511.